AFTER GOYA

&

New

Selected Poems

Roger Aplon

Dedicated to all those who continue the fight

for Enlightenment & Freedom

Wherever & Whenever

Contents

Selected Poems: Encounters

The Birth of Zoe & Noa

Contemplation & Memory – New York to DC
For Jason & Ivana

On the train to DC the loose litter from last night's rain
scatters through the tunnels & over the lagoons
that mark the southern route from New York City.

In the first photos Ivana beams & cuddles her tiny bundles,
two days birthed, the living earth enhanced by two,
the mind of the viewer grasping for the right words.

Unnerving in its simplicity yet shrouded in mystery,
this birth, this most natural act challenges
our accepted scale of time & continuum.

& as we pass Philadelphia I'm reminded of a trip many years ago:

I'd hitchhiked east from Chicago the proverbial *seeker after truth* an escapee from an intimidating dad. One night, sleeping under a viaduct with others who'd chosen this place for safety and seclusion, we were awakened by a man moaning. Two of us found him bleeding from a gash in his head and clutching a baby wrapped in a nearly clean blanket. We fixed the man as best we could with iodine and gauze – the hitchhiker's first-aid kit. He told a story of abandoned kids, of rescue, of the choices, *at that time,* women had to make. How he (*his words*) 'wrestled the devil to the ground' and paid the price. We decided to take the baby to a firehouse we'd passed. The old guy was too weak to argue and actually seemed relieved to be free of his burden. The firemen were equally pleased – said they'd rather see them healthy and alive than not.

About an hour out of DC I can't but reflect on that time &
the horror of those unwanted & abandoned & . . . of Zoe & Noa
safely cradled in the arms of their mom & their dad.

The rotation of the earth seems a hair quicker, the sky a touch crisper,
the birches bordering the track this fall day incendiary in their applause.

Vermeer @ The Prado

The house is dark but light through the window tells the time &
brings a shine to the young woman's face & to the guitar she strokes.

Notice the map of the known world above the table & the
lowered eyes of the darker girl who holds an empty glass &

the crafty grin of the man in black who insists on pouring more
wine & the clown at the window who chuckles & waggles his
tongue & . . .

In the upper room, even darker now, the doctor has come to test
their mother's pulse & like the hunter with his bag of game,
leaves something to remember,

maybe a pheasant-cock to be plucked or maybe he's come to
deliver a letter from an admirer – who can say?

After all, it's the painter who has let the fruit fall on the bed &
turned the death-mask face-up on the table &

It's also the painter with his back turned who studies the girl &
her downcast eyes, the pale dog who wanders between them,
determines

when to open the window & where the light will go & how the
night will end for the women & the men who prowl these rooms looking

for the book that will tell them, for the glass that will lead them,
for the door that will open out & set them free.

A Film In Three Acts

1

Where the mist parts above the falls the figure of a man is framed
against the horizon & coming our way.

Must we send a messenger to meet him?

He, who is spoken of in private, the one whose people swore
pain on our house?

Who do we trust to carry our word or speak our names? These
are days of reunion. We must not forget.

2

It was dark by six & no sign of either the man or our messenger.
At eight we sat for dinner.

Martha spoke of her mother's wake & the people covered in straw.
Many invited did not attend.

At the cemetery, under a hazy moon, two figures wrestle in the snow.
Behind the courthouse a hanged man twists in the wind

3

To awake is to settle the score
& escape the inevitable.

By the time he responded
    there was nothing left to lose.

As he reaches to lift his mask the sky opens.
    There are clawing birds & the acrid pall of death.

Reflections

He can only be seen in the distance. Contemplating
(or so we imagine) his years of evading encounters.
It was his way. Those who came too close were excluded.

Like Linda who flew from Saskatchewan to meet him
only to be told their time had passed. Or Charmayne
who lay waiting in Madrid & received a small note:
Surprise is not welcome & neither are you.

It was the same for his father – dedicated to survival or
was it a preoccupation with outwitting destiny
with its layers of subterfuge, random misery & loss of control?

In the quiet time, before sunset, you might find him puttering
among the flotsam & jetsam of a life in tumult – where
the word "trust" was always embarrassingly out-of-reach,
where one mistake could fracture expectations or explode a dream.

The future contains the present & the past. Like Monarch butterflies
that never return home but arm their kids with memories of time
& place – a map of hope & desire to entice & fortify against
failure.

Aras

Music of Senegal

Each takes his turn as is the style of jazz & the players of Aras
corral their women & their men to dance &

small kids slip away to watch & a chance to join / except the one
who misses her mother's teat & strains to suck &

her blouse is open & night closes in & the music insinuates &
first one lithe woman leaps & kicks her heels & the next &

up & back they push & stride & the drummer caresses & the
drummer whacks & the drummer strikes his clever strokes &

the kora player twitches & twangs & peaks & slides & hums &
sings & the moon climbs the Cedars & the fragile bougainvillea &

across the aisle a woman strokes her lover's arm & I lean to
you, as is the custom, & kiss you, as is the custom &

the room sways in unison to the rhythm & call as stalk by stalk &
limb by limb the lavender petals rise & fall.

The Leap

After: Jean-Marc Superville Sovak's 'enhancement' of J Conser's 19th
Century Lithograph

Lake George appears calm
below the surface an unpredictable current . . .

Schooner rounding a bend / Small sail making way
On the distant beach
a dozen or so black men & black women have come together
hopeful of their crossing into Canada
In the foreground a dingy bearing several more
One hails the lone girl on the cliff above

I will not hesitate. I will not be stopped. I will be strong. I will be . . .

careful of loose gravel
set yourself on the ledge
(she waves to those who wait below)
they say the lake's plenty deep
fix your eyes on the distant sky
don't look down

Mama's last words echo:
"This be your turn. This be your time. Your forebears will guide you. I will
guide you.
You never be alone."

O K
&
Here she goes

. . .

A woman
hurtles from the cliff
terrified
skirt billowing
exalted
arms outstretched

Knowing
(as water parts under her weight)
She has survived & . . . Yes

she will be
going
on

Poem For Debra On Her Birthday

8-27-2014

Crossing the Mason-Dixon Line
heading due south
there you are
musical notes crowding out
mom's terror, new work
still germinating,
the trials of dreams
roiling further down
the road where
the mind plays its lethal tricks – Yes
It always comes back
to that: Music &
how you treat your gift, sometimes
earnestly, sometimes
tenderly – not
unlike the conductor with her baton,
commanding discipline
with one stroke &
free improvisation with the next . . . & as
your plane settles back
to earth, the reality
of your birth (or might it be rebirth)
speaks of past & future,
our annual
connection with our destiny, yours
to choose: the red stone
or the white,

to entreat the music to sing to you, that
communal song of renewal,
as only it can,
to choose the road to the mountain's top
& the sylvan lake
that awaits
all who are willing & brave & filled
with love of life & living
like you

Happy Birthday

Out Of The Night

The woman steps out of her box & loses herself in the weeds
The man rides to meet her where the fallen lie in wait

In time she'll wake to see the sun again – as was foretold. & He
with his empty pack & inspired by her music
expects nothing.

Where they met is not important, Goodwill or Grace Church,
who remembers? It's where they'll go that matters. Yes?
& how – As has been warned:

Ignite a luster in the blood or find it bleak as wheat in the rain,
handfuls of bristles, too soft to hold,
too bitter to swallow.

It's a simple choice – troubling for the naïve, uninitiated & them,
from one continent to another, did not – but gorged
on leftovers & lies, begging for

the magician with his sacred cards, the poet with his furious words,
the priest or seer or prophet – someone to expiate
their years of drought.

We know it's never someone else: Truth is best revealed in
dreams, theirs are indicative: His: a terrified Corgi swallowed
by a Python – Hers: the river in flames,

no wind, no stars, no open fields . . . Their last frame only hints
at conciliation . . . while opportunity
rumbles away – oblivious.

*The healer with his magic wand is dead. Long live the healer.
Long live the ghost of hope, the bearer of chance,
the pastor of transformation.*

When Sleep Is Not An Option

In this dream I round your corner with a basket of eels & you
curse my name & brandish your silver gun &

it's then I remember an old & precious melody – it's 'Take The
A Train' & I do, as far as the river & there's a man dressed as a
clown in

oversized shoes, baggy pants & a big red nose, who calls me by
my mother's name & points to you poised to dive at the edge of
the pier &

I catch the next train to the bowery where you're already waiting
on the subway stairs & massaging the neck of the conductor & here

night closes in & there's the man with his pack of black dogs dividing
the profits from his game of 'catch the pony in the dark' &

there's another clown dressed all in blue who rings a bell &
decorates a table with lilies & belladonna & when the waiter
arrives with his shovel & broom

I try to slip you a taste of your favorite chocolate but you're too
far down the track & running headlong into the headlights

A Wet Afternoon

A wet afternoon recalls the image of a small boy riding his
bicycle with wet newspapers to deliver to a home where they're
soon trashed &

in the next frame on another wet afternoon he's driving a
grocer's truck & the load is lettuce & roast beef & we find him

in bed with a girl who is wet & knows more than he about wet
afternoons & rolls over to show him how &

a winter goes by & another & in a thunderstorm he's sweating
under a canoe in Wisconsin when Diane offers her hand & her
wet mouth &

it's ten years later & he & Julia are driving through mist to the
mountain & the rainbow that is their final run at hope &

today, on this wet afternoon, he's no longer a kid & shuffles his
collection of photos to find the one of her under the umbrella &

how wet she could be on any day or night when the fire crackled
& Noche, the cat, curled on their hearth & . . . & it ends here

with an empty bottle & a loaded gun & when the rain comes
again it will just be rain & no place to run

Just-Like-That

The valley floor heaves & rumbles as rain cascades & lightning
chases them to their king-size bed where he slips

into her & panthers race the sky & coyotes scream with their
ghosts swimming through mesquite & cactus &

tongues entwine & mouths seek the tender crevasses & she
hugs him closer, loving the startling

rage of the thunder & rolls out her own siren song, long & loud
& he whispers an urgent *'Wait'* & finches

erupt from the pines, the maverick loon parts the cattails & she
flies-up like Chagall's bride & wrestles

his big red fish, tucks his violin under her chin & *just-like-that*
she's gone.

A Story In One Movement

*. . . the sexual libido becomes rampant in the Existential Vacuum
Viktor Frankl:* <u>Man's Search For Meaning</u>

She came in the night, bearing her secret life & promises of un-bridled sex with whomever she chose. Her idea was to keep three lights lit, flying from one hot bulb to the next without being scorched or even working up a sweat. To her the game of musical beds was how to pass time while waiting to die. She'd come through here before & reminded us of those elastic nights she could stretch tight as a drum's head or a cock's foreskin on Viagra. Having her back meant the willows will weep no more, the barflies thirst no longer, the storytellers plates are filled. She took the rooms over Moriarty's saloon & spent the first night with the lean dark busboy from Morocco. That was Tuesday. By Friday she'd savored the flesh up & down the bar that included men & women. From the buzz in the place it seems her favorite position was that of the receptive hound & her favorite sport was straddling her partner's face while he or she hummed on her whistle. This is not to say she didn't play assorted games too numerous to list in such short space. Suffice to say she made her mark & just before leaving our startled community took this writer to the sack – a night he'll never forget & has herpes & bite-marks to prove it. That was September. Scuttlebutt had her traveling between Paris & Barcelona or Tangiers & Bethlehem it didn't seem to matter which. In the Daily Mirror we read she'd married the Prince & is taking holiday on his mother's yacht in the Aegean. Months passed before we heard again. This time it was a phone call to my neighbor, Doctor Font, requesting the address of a laboratory that specialized in snake venom.

Selected Poems: To Witness

Trusting Intuition

Her gun explodes. Bicycle in the oak tree. Jack-knifed semi. Junk bonds. Beware the benevolent. Rummage & Renovate. Ten quick steps. Solitude. Be damned. With or without. He must isolate the father. Freedom at any price. Quit robbing Peter to pay your poodle. Home. Hearth. Gather & dismantle. Whatchagonnadonow? Teeth on fire. Tucumcari. Too much to hope for. Outta yur mind. Up we go. The father – yes! Set you down this . . . Rolling & her wild ride. Upstairs. Uppity. Unplanned. Unprepared. Whatever-it-takes. What there is to discover. What there is to save – to lose – to disown. Listen. Never before. Chow Mein. Candlesticks. Quonset hut. Abracadabra. & if that's not enough . . . Subterfuge. Ransack. Ruminate. Right hook. Weatherman. Wouldn't you know? One by one by two. Discrepancy. Nowhere to run nowhere to hide. The body. If not today, when? Time enough . . . Say it ain't so. Superfine. Salt in the wound. Purple heart. Broken heart. Castigate. Crawlspace. Turpentine. Like the man said. There comes a time. Don't talk. What are we waiting for? Some things . . . Sometime. Where's a mother when you need one? Sacrosanct. & that makes nine. Mighty-fine. Buns & butter. Beware. Be Square. Behind the door. Up Up & Away. It pays to . . . What'd you say? Gotta Go. What'd you mean? Gotta go. Down the Up staircase. Settle a score. Store a kettle. It won't bring her back. Rattlesnakes. Chocolate cake. & what's it to you? Speak your mind. From one to the other. Nonchalance. For the greater good. Would. Should. Could. Once upon . . . He's still alive. Still kicking. Still unmoved. Still can't believe. Iceberg. Butterscotch. Beneath. Beside. Below. Gifted. Gopher. Be still. Silly me. One more round. One more quick & clever. It don't mean so much now. & so it goes

Black Granite White Mirror
Viet Nam Memorial Wall - Washington, DC - 1982

Dear Leonard,
It's been 22 years since they took you & all our beautiful
boys & girls.
What generous children they might have been. Like you,
Len, dead, like you.

———

Beside its gripping litany of names this wall's been home to cards
& letters, snapshots, whiskey, dolls & bibles . . . telephones &
purple hearts . . . &

once – to living vets - their outfit's badges, caps & battle flags
laid out across the lawn, just down the hill from Lincoln.

Those who still come from Omaha & Chillicothe, Chicago,
Orlando, Duke or Sacramento seek their peace in its slick, dark skin.

Their hands, their eyes, their passing shadows linked to all
who've walked this walk
before.

After more than thirty-eight years this wall is still a door / an
entrance to the other side of grief

those who've gone ahead forever joined – the living & the dead
as flesh to bone . . . as skin to stone.

There's A Hole That Cannot Be Filled

There's a hole in the hall & another in the door that leads to the bedroom &
another in the kitchen &

in fact, there are holes throughout this house & the garden is filled
with holes &

there are holes in the visions of those who live here & thrive on
empty spaces &

their neighbors & their kids & the neighbor's kids & the gardeners
& mechanics & bartenders all thrive

on the emptiness that buys them time & an official calm that offers
success &

out of the holes come the rabid dogs & rats & a plague of spiders
& no one seems to mind

as long as the weather be good & there're trains to ride & the
news only plays once & only at Ten.

The Shades In America Are Down

Summer has taken its toll & one by one
couples abandon their rooms & move to the mountains or the sea or

wherever families gather for the last hot nights &
they sweat together under the weight of vagabonds & tramps & pick-

pockets & the larvae of the street who swarm
in their dreams like adolescents intent on shame & they welcome

the relief of a cool bath
to alter their thinking & only wish for salvation from debts & fear &

for simple pleasures: a place to hide
their memories of blood being spilled & the chill of the dead alone

on a carpet of tears & promise
to recollect forgotten promises & come home to the usual business:

bury their head in the sand &
lift their asses high enough to be noticed by those politicians who relish

a good fucking of the willingly ignorant & uninformed.

On Moving The Immoveable

His rhinestone studded frog appears as a panther about to strike,
his flowering cactus wants to tattoo its imprint on his bare back,
one pill in the morning is not enough to chase the nagging boil in his belly.

It's been like this for more than a month. Nothing seems willing
to change: not his unwavering yearning for calm or his insistent
warring with clutter & impatience with all news of the daddy in charge.

This isn't a simple Oedipal obsession as much as it is reaction to
the grinding gears in his head, the torment of loose bowels or the
evidence of rats in the kitchen. No. This is unfettered distress

after two years of watching the locomotive run amuck – tolerat-
ing temperature's collapse to sixty-degrees below zero over three
quarters of the country or ICE poised to pounce on the slightest
among us,

all this tasteless video footage – enough to terrify even a hard-
assed mother-in-law, cop or killer – what will it take to finally
dismantle the death-star we've aligned ourselves with in our
naïve pursuit of freedom.

The Knee

The knee on the neck of George Floyd
is a knife in the heart
of those ideals
we claim
as our

sac

red

he

r

i

t

a

g

e

May 25, 2020 - U S A

8 8

The chosen tattoo of the faithful

Note: H is the eighth letter of the alphabet – Hence 88: the anagram for
Heil Hitler

They raise their straight-arms in their malevolent salute – Replicated over & over in bars, in secret enclaves, in schools, in churches, in the streets & alleys of *his* blood-soaked wonderland of maimed or dead Niggers, Kikes & Rag-Heads.
With each gesture, each assault, every thrust of their blade, every blow of their bats they honor the memory of their savior, their general, their mentor & guide to these fetid fields of ethnic purity –

Heil Hitler

proclaimed in their rush to emulate, to praise, to decimate, to gouge-out any trace of *'The Other'* – The dark side of their vision, of their alternative universe, where only blond-white supplicants are welcome. All hail the supreme, the chosen, the righteous, the sinister, the strange & estranged – All who march in the boot-prints of Ein Führer & those who worship at his feet. Yes. We know you. For what you are. For what you are not. Soon, your enabler will be but scum on the pond of history & you will return to the shadows where you fume & fester. But . . . Mark This:
When you once more slither from under your rock
We will be waiting.

The Sculpted Visions Of Olafur Eliasson

As The Iraq War Enfolds

I walk across this field of cinders & ash & through his mirrored
passage all tilted & fractured, into the room that swims in smoke &

here I lie on the bed that maps the course of time & place &
dream of the thick-lipped vagina in the tree that has been torched
& it's skin peeled back &

wait for word of the other mutations & mutilations that mount as
the day grows colder & death waits in the wings like a pale bird
crouched on the lawn

where I wake to the seductive whispers of a woman in a yellow
blouse with a camera who's come to freeze this trance in time . . .
But – there is no way

to capture what will not wait as the tanks come faster & the
drone of the planes grows louder & the bombs & the fires,

that attend that moment, break the will of the sculptor who
wanders from room to room with his chisel & broom &

fills the bath with iodine & swims out where there are no hooks
& the fish are free & the mermaid in green

is all he will ever remember of that day.

Madrid, Spain
For Judy

Love In The Time Of Jihad

It's said, decapitation is preferable. Decisive. No questions remain. Jail, a poor alternative: secret messages, collusion, escapes.

*

There are no rats where he sleeps. They are a food-source after all. Today, it's amplified sound, piercing & penetrating – Today, it comes in waves.

With each inquisition the tension grows. Last week was a broken arm. Will the next be terminal? . . . who can tell?

*

Would she come?
                    Will she forget?
                                        Like the last time?

*

Shifting his whip from hand to hand the master gestures for the rocks to rain down, driven by

fear & passion, driven by an eagerness to please their God & he who holds the book.

*

Forgetting the dark is easy. It's the silence. The silence & time . .
. that's the hardest part – Time. It crawls – It stutters – It snaps
the reins.

*

Before the whispered threats, they played backgammon in the
bunker, before the ivory dice & the bloody knife . . . There are
no bargains

in the bazaar, no secret passageways for fugitives. One muffled
shout & the lights go out. Prayer. Prayer is all that's left. Or so
it's thought.

*

If he makes it to Sunday there's a slim chance for conciliation –
The world has come to his door & there is no one home.

*

They've been at it for twenty minutes. In the haze & heat of the
day, her blood has dried a dull brown on the egg-shaped stones.

It's time for a break & a smoke. They will be summoned again.
It's left to him who leads them, him, who deals the cards.

*

She will not come.
> *She has not forgotten.*
>> *This was the last time.*

Sabotage

He's fourteen & green. she's his teacher & he's the one who
stands out.

Sap his strength –
That's the way.
Squash his ego –
That's the way.
Make him grovel . . . After all, you hold the reins.

Someone's erected a plaque to those who survived.
No blood spilled. No.
But.
Deeply felt –
Accused –
Ignored –
Diminished.

How many years? Did it take?
If any ever came? For revival?
Where there was a bud, a shriveled stem . . . heart, mind & spirit
work as one:

Alcohol? For Sure. Drugs? Passive or active. Yes. & Mayhem?
Possibly. &
All those wasted years.

Easy for them. To ask,

"Who was your favorite?" Or "Who was the most influential?" Never:

"Who was the one Destroyed your love
        of learning –
Debilitated your sense
        of self-worth?"

Stars align in sequence.
One step forward & a double-step back.
*Can't get nowhere
 fast or slow.*

No. Not like that. No.

Not crippled –
Not crippled like that.

Desert Lullaby

Remembering (Among So Many) the Hass Refugee Camp – Idlib, Syria – 8/16/2019

Yes Tonight A camp Initiated for the Safety & Health of the Disoriented Displaced & Dislodged Lies silent only Fragments of Bodies that Once Filled its Squalid Tents Remain & Yes as Reported a Bomb From a Lone Russian Jet Dissolved All Hope of Life With a Whimper & a Bang & So Yes We Announce & Plead We're So Sick of War & The Thugs Who Bank Their vigorish Their *juice* From Loans They make to Allay the Risk of Peace & the Loss of Planes that Mysteriously Explode or Tanks that Rocket to Incendiary Mush or a Bomb that Eludes its Target or a Battalion Over-Run & Slaughtered Yes Our small voices Ring Hollow In the Desert Yes In the Mountains Yes In these City Streets Yes In the Fat Council Halls & Dusty Huts where Generals Plan the Next & the Next & the Next Yes & Yes & Yes. We Implore Once More *our hollow cry* We Are So Sick Of War

As My Prisoner Ages

It's no longer an exercise in torture. That ended years ago.
The pain of incarceration is far subtler:
days & nights spent sifting through soiled linen, he wanders
the compound like a hapless joke
anticipating applause that will never come.
I've learned to ignore
his yearning for Bourbon before noon,
his trembling at the mirror as his beard whitens & his thinning
hair falls.

Coloring his nights,
the replay of Ellen's suicide, her blood soaking through
their newly installed Berber carpet,
her dream of a new home blown away by her own hand & his
Smith & Wesson '38 Mag.
As the years have tumbled by what might be has morphed to
what might have been fueled by the image
of the hobbled horse awaiting the lion's leap.
Horny but fearful of impotence
he surfs the web for porn,
masturbates before he dozes-off, accomplishes
as little as possible.

Beware Of Prophesies

& promises that flare in the dark like shimmering beacons, like
dreams of perfection only a child can imagine.

*

*On days like this, I remember mother rolling her dough,
slicing the tart apples I'd pick from the tree in the yard, how
she'd fill the pan, dust with brown sugar, unfold the dough to
cover & prick the holes.*

*

Last night, his actions spoke of dementia, the flourish of a knife in
one hand,
your throat in the other, how he spit in your face
when you tried to kiss the blade?

*

*Her crust was the flakiest, the lightest, the most memorable
of my young life when danger never threatened & each day
began with the cooing of the mourning doves that nested in
the pines across the field & . . .*

*

These are the days revealed in his letters. Remember your oath.
Locked or open, the door is still a door & swings both ways. You
are your own best friend & . . .

*

Outside, in the garden, a pair of hummingbirds dip & dive, swoop & disappear . . . where the honeysuckle blooms bees & ants compete. The hummingbirds return for another pass . . . trumpet vine & lilac &.

*

Take *The Limited* south. Tell me you're safe, that the migrating Monarchs & Martins still fill the sky. I'll come in the spring & . . ... if

In Their Wake

In parts of the Orient bats serve as symbols of good luck, long
life, and happiness.

In their wake a fine rain & a common hunger at sundown. All
else remains the same: twin retrievers

tethered to a boy's memory of subterfuge & sabotage, a war he
could never win, his father, all business &

armed against metaphor, his mother a shadow in the pantry
dishing castor oil, wilted spinach & Thursday's liver.

Their wake is calm. He pauses for one last look & a nap at the
water's edge. It's impossible

to separate the rising tide from their passing. I walk with it daily
as we all must if we've survived.

& the bats? Who will manage their nourishment or corner their
fury? They enter their weather at full speed

as if they have no time for council or remorse, as if they've been
warned of loss & cautioned

don't look back.

Six New Improvisations

Improvisation – To Remind You

To tell you how it was. To remind you. Why. Inauguration. Or not. No matter. Remember. That other time. You with the pistol. She with her purple wig & Bowie knife. When crossing borders it's best. A secret hidden. Underwear. Watch cap. Maps. Toilet paper. Chewing gum. Grumbling in the walls. Thunderbird in flight. Here. Hold the reins. Whisper Chipper. Chomp-Chomp. Be that as it may. Brother. Can you spare a dime? What time is it? Carry on. You'll be missed. Never. Trouble in paradise. With or without. Fancy that. & so it goes. One hand washing the other. Mother's eyes. Sister Mary in her finest. Forget the keys? There's more than you'll ever know. Steal the show. Snow job. Salt of the earth. Quonset. Descent. Domicile. Run, jump, spin. Take the B train. When waves broke over the breakwater. After dinner. Before Church. Underground. Sure thing. Nonsense. Never trust on luck. Buck the trend. Devour angst. Think Sunnyside. Bye-bye. Fly by. Fiddle or not, here we come. It was not expected. His is a tale worth remembering. Polish the apple. Out of the dark. Into the light. Never trust a fat man smoking a Meerschaum pipe. Lights out. No time to waste. No time to flay the cat or burn the mountain down. One by one & two by two. & so it goes.

Improvisation – Where The Rivers Meet

Be watchful. There. Where the rivers meet. Release the caged wolverine, the scorpions & hooded cobras. Time is your mistress. Bring her a hot sweet-roll & coffee. Kiss her on both cheeks & remind her of your love. Beware the man who rides the whirlwind, he who bridles the stallion in the yard. Collect his fractured dreams. Order his sentries to the four gates. Unbolt the basement door before the moon rises & the bats are free. This is your cue to exit. Remember your keys & water for the road. Before it's too late, forget the lost briefcase, the maps & ironed shirts. Once you're in the wind, repeat the lessons learned & actions taken. The mystery left to solve is the one you carry in your black pouch. There will be a signpost & an owl to guide you. Those of us who have gone before salute you. Our praise is not enough. You must take back what was misplaced. As the sun rises so shall you. Bend to your task. What lies behind you is not our question or our concern. Where the rivers meet, under the Banyan Tree, under the rock, you'll find the box & all you will need of revelations. Here, at the edge, the scent of lilac & sage. Take a deep breath. Reach up. Step out & open your arms.

Improvisation - On A Saturday Afternoon In July #1

Hot to trot to hop to lunge the Quaker's got your name sir. Wise up. Can't play dead. Readers awake. A moribund afternoon in May. Days of our lives. A raft on a cool afternoon. Wake up. Yes. You. No time left. A wonder indeed. Keep it coming. Got the rhythm? Got the juice? Spoken like a true & cruel patriot. & why not. Come on. Be better than you think you are. What's the matter? Lose your orphaned twin? Get along now. No Loitering. No time for strangers. Wrap the fish to go. A bouquet of violets for the lonely & the brave. Say. Wasn't that your neighbor's wife I saw you with. What a surprise. Thought she was dead. Only looks that way. & say. Wasn't that your kid on the evening news? The story about rape & pillage & war on the street? I could have sworn. No matter. He was someone's dontchaknow. & like that, he's gone. Up the chimney in a whiff. Of smoke & who comes poking around but his sister with the wooden leg. Poor baby. Here. I'll take you in. You must be hungry. After all this time. Just rest your swollen head on my chest. Slurp your hot soup. Wanna dance? Hip/hop / Ziplock. Snap Snap. & blat de blat blat . . . music to my ears. Pure, lost & wet as Wednesday . . .

Improvisation - On A Saturday Afternoon In July #2

Out of the dark. Tom-Tom bugle & the raspy weather. Tone on tone. The marchers pass by. Weighted down with worry & work & the wonder of it all. Like Magic. Tone on tone. Double down. Follow the money. Many have gone before. Where were you when Henry . . .? Drop the silver in the slot. The train's ready. Pulling out. A fast hand swipes across the moon. Pleasing as it may seem. The mule's broken loose. Hold up. They're trying to come aboard. Whittle down the scale. Make room for the balloons. Better you then me. Dontchasee. Running ahead. One by one. Two by two. It's a circus out there. See the clowns & elephants & even a tiger or two? Where will it lead? Too late for marriage. Take what you can. The clothes on your back. Bodies in the road. Forget what came before. Run now. To the left. To the right. Don't look back Jack. Here. Here I am. Maria. You too. Wait. There's not enough room. Bury the fat cat in the furry hat. Be prepared. I can see the end of the road. There's a copperhead & two dancing bears. Where's your sense of humor? Buy a forty-five & blow 'em away. Hey. Gotta quarter for the kitty? Whitey will turn the other cheek. Sneak a peek. Bumble-bee. Stumblebum. A rhyme in time. Ta-ta. Ta-ta. For all that. Ta-ta. Ta-ta. For all that. & so it goes.

Legacy

I E D. Gas mask. Rocket launcher. Humvee. Bumble Bee. Vocation. Vacation. & who's to tell? Vivisection. Victory. Vaccination. & who's to say? & why not? Here come the two by two's. Four by four's. Fortunes to win & Fortunes to lose. Mark one for the displeased. & one for the dispossessed. Chattel. Skedaddle. Once, on the Panama Limited . . . Porterhouse. Vacant house. Housebound. House on fire. Separation. Sequester. Blood in the eye. Blown away. Quadriplegic. Ordinary crimes. Without offence. Always ready for more. Who says? OK by me. Remember your first time. How the blood surged. How the sweat ran down your back. Fingers froze. From dune to dune. & him without his cock & balls. Blood dries dark brown in this heat. & fast too. & me without my rubbers. Shape up cowboy. Ride 'im girl. From one to the next. Coordinates. A bolt is loose. Map this. Up yours. From one asshole to another. Outta my face. Sackcloth & Ashes. Swollen. & where's his face? Back home. On the swing. Over the BBQ. Hovering. Smothering. Jostling troubadours. When the smoke clears. Armor & sweat. Sweat & armor. Semper Fi. Down the drain. Thunder & rain.

There's Never Enough Truth Or Enough Justice . . .

Squandered. Relished. Radioactive. Reverse field. Run amuck. River of random. & what does she have to say? Hey. Why the warfare? Why the drizzle in the dream? Speak of demeanor. Sculpture. Savagery. Succulence. & here the boat stops. Recompense. Flotilla of angst. Symmetry. Sloe gin. Seventh-day-Adventists. Mercury. Monosyllabic. Mary-Jane. Mother-in-law. Red necks. Rolling paper. Out of the woods. Coming close. Not what it seemed. All of a sudden. Quadriceps. On the move. What & why not? Who's to say? & Who will carry the day? & Who has the balls? & Whether or not. Slumber. Solitude. Somewhere. Somehow. Sometime. Behind bars. Under the stairs. Between the sheets. Wrath & Wonder. Rolling Thunder. Here's to solutions. & here's to digging deeper. & here's to ready or not. One man's curse. One man's salvation. One for one & one for all. & so it goes. Treading heavy. Over the stones. Through the new mown grass. Over graves that speak of wisdom & folly run amuck. Torment & torture. Surly you'll not comply. & Why? Sail on silver bird. O'Casey, "Be Brave. Be Brave. & Evermore Be Brave." Run with the wolves. Feast with lions. Sacrifice. Stillborn. Suspicious. For all we know. Swallows wheel & whine & tilt the sky. Gavel. Whip. Chain. Who will cast the first stone. Eye for an Eye. Bitter. Sweet. Ride the clouds. Bareback & Bountiful. Cattle prod. Pick & shovel. Rack & ruin. Hangman's hood & Hangman's knot. Last Hurrah. Guillotine & Cyanide. Welcome. All is forgiven. Home. For all it's worth. Snake-Eyes.

Celebrating The Free Musical Improvisations of Anthony Tan

Reminiscence

After Anthony Tan's Endlessnessnessnessnessness

It's coming. The tide. & you fight it & it comes & you can't stop it & here the voices hover like trombones or are they hammers & flutes & one by the one the gamblers stumble & stagger through the drapes that flap against the house on the hill where maps are drawn & fires lit & he plays his harmonica & wrestles his demons from Amsterdam or Swaziland or Timbuctoo & monumental waves uproot the coast with their brass-knuckles & Gatling-Guns & heave & ho & here comes Robin with the queen of spades & her glowing obsidian niece & out go the lights in the tower & streaming ribbons of smoke slither here & there & everywhere & another corpse & hay-wagons filled to the brim with salt-peanuts & caviar & machetes & meat hooks where the scur-rying rats & monkeys gouge & dance & here's the rain & torrents of sour mash & our cousins from Detroit & Black Bottom Rum & One-Eyed Jacks & Aces High & *Whatdoyouknow* spouting gibberish & Maryann with bucket & chisel & the hand of the master-batter & Cops & Aldermen & "I-Can't-Breathe" & buckets & hangers & welts on each cheek before the ramp is lowered & out of the dark run the thirty we thought were lost & so it went that day when not a drop of blood was spilled to save one slave or was it a slaver or who knows for sure & no records were kept & babies cried & succotash & "Please Don't" & "She's not yet twelve" & Voila It's Daisy Mae & the Lone Ranger & *who-the-hell-cares* & rubbadubdub & Marian Indiana & out-of-the-dark "There's the Nigger" & the rope & the tree & one-after-another the butchers & bearers & the crowd cheers & there's enough of that to go around & one by one & two by two & an axe-handle here & a buggy whip there & some drove all night & others swilling Old

Crow in the half-light & the stink of sweat & vomit & after it's over
the sweepers come & that's all we'll know of that time & that place &
those who came & those who went & those who did not.

Landscape

After Anthony Tan's Ksana II

His gnarly squirrels scurry up one tree & down the other & mothers smother their kids with love & the squeaking door whistles for those who've come to meditate on *"Advice & Sound of Mutilation"* & from behind the screen the horn-a-plenty rears its obnoxious head while three naked boys skim the pond for algea to eat & something safe to drink & Anthony whips the players & rides his baton & a tiger snarls & a bull bellows & tap-tap-tap from the basement where *one-after-the-other* ricochets & threatens & the train whistles & the gates heave & the gates collapse & in the distance a pack of hyenas & on the horizon blue smoke & a flag & the rumble of wagons & low flying jets & worming its way from under the house two broken legs on a stretcher & a medic with cap & gown & on another the scarred torso of a woman & from the valley a cello & the buzz of cicadas & the crackle of brush-on-fire & a startled scream & footsteps on the stairs & a black hawk with a rat in its talons & no one speaks of the night ahead & no one speaks of the days behind & no one's left to imagine what cannot be told.

After Anthony Tan's *'Observing the Ph(r)ase'*

Climbing out he stoops to tie his shoe & wonders & waits & there's lust too. He's driving over a bridge & it's Louisiana & the bridge tilts & the road twists & he's falling into the zone below & . . . & there's a pause here & sirens & spectators cheer & a brown dog's running & someone bangs a pot & another a pan & the trigger is pulled & the gun goes off & they're rummaging to the center & the dog's a giraffe & there're lawyers & hand-grenades & alley-oop & ringadingding & out of the dark his shadow turns & they're dancing as only a man & his shadow can & dolphins rise & the moon too & under it all a quivering mass of fingers & toes & remember to write & he says he will & forgets to remove his boots & the whip he's stuffed in his belt & stars explode & the blindman wags his bony finger & the curtain too & the clowns run-out in rags & muffins & here's where he makes his last stand & it's only the beginning & there're moths & rye whiskey & rooms for rent & a cattle-call & the play begins & bodies hang from lampposts & the singer forgets his lines & Baby-Ruth & Mumbly-Peg & who's got the knife & who'd got the time & watch this & he does & a wave takes the pier out to sea & him with it & he trips over his shoelace & the trap is spring & he owns the dice & throws snake-eyes & a bell rings & he's brushing his teeth with earwax & one-by-one the runners pass & he hands each a number & a cup & when he looks-up the moon blinks back & there's nowhere to turn & nowhere to hide & he does as he's always done & that will have to do – Or – so it seems – for now . . .

Tic Tic Tic

After Anthony Tan's. *"OntheSensationsofTone"*

& Hit it! Catch the wave. Zero in. We'll go first. & here come the insidious, the rambling, the courageous inducements. This way is plagued. Like scattered rice. There's more than one. Watch out! It's catching. Worrisome. This deafening. This absolute. End. Wait! Watch for the descending curse. You're bound to mistake the last. Where are the kids? Going? Wait! The screen's covered with moths. They wander in the mind. Behold. Contrary. Lost ground. You're in route. There's no escape. Wait! One after the other. They come. One carries a banana. One carries the next in line. They stumble. They always. Stumble. No remorse. Wait! Some say you've crossed over. Others laugh. Behind your back. Who can you trust? Not him with the tainted grin. Not him with the bushy tail. Not him with the screwed caboose. Cringe & the world cringes. Fight or die in the breach. On the beach. Can't get started. Try oatmeal. An apple a day. Sugarplums. Wait! There's more than howling. In the eaves. Truckloads of broken promises. Trainloads of broken bodies. Around every corner another corner. Who will stop the churning? The wavering? The hopeless sobbing? & here they conclude. One with his shirt on fire / The other with her dress undone. Where will they meet? It's written. Somewhere. For sure. No characters left to mask the graves. He rants into the tube & flushes it. Think. Crazy. Think. Random acts of solicitation. Pick one & the rest will disintegrate. It's not your turn. Your way out. Your train's running late. Wait. She's mouthing something. Freedom. Who remembers. Who to trust? Who will be next. A Quantum leap. Spaghetti. Spangles. Slippers & a slap in the face. Wait! Baboons. Buckets. Balloons. Red's my choice. Say it isn't so. Say it's not your fault. Wait! One by one the runners. Two by two the rats & ravens. Wish me luck. I've come this far. Don't be late.

Don't bother. Send for help. There's never enough to go around. It's the time we live. Not so different than the time we didn't. Don't apologize – Don't complain. Forever dedicated. Forever blind. Forever without purpose. Just like that last time. Just like magic. They swarm & then they're gone.

After: Anthony Tan's

Un/Divided

Humm – Humm – Humm & gatt & got & gaunt & got gaunt & She breathes & He gasps & dit & dit & dot-dot & catch & wire on fire & eery & envy & tink & tingle & mum & mum & mum & boc & book & botch & up & down & here's the weather & the Giant whispers & Yes & Yes & gasps & gaps & guppies & goop & careful where you tread & groan & Oh & mute & mutant & night slips away like cancer in the blood & round & round & Bam & Bam & Oh my Ga . . . & Down the Up into oblivion - into stargaze - into water-bucket & whoops & "Who's There?" & Squeaky clean & Squeaky nuggets & full rush ahead & Oh No & gasp & gasp & gasp & bute & boot & aga & gaga & it's cold in here & whiskey-walnuts-run-why-dontcha? & Hunger & a clipped laugh & goo & gog & shuuuuush & up & down & here it comes / Straight at you & Bam & Pang & Pong & Push the music & grapple & grumble & piercing & dit & dat & he sucks on his pipe & blood in the eye & a sharpened axe & cut the cord & the door what will not open open open open – NoT & NoT & Noise & Nose & the trio against the wall & fireflies & a kiss under the willow & the weeping kid & jerked chicken & time without measure & Yikes & Ike & ick & stick & sticky & savvy & toothpicks & the voice between us & rattle my cage & guess what? & who's to say & one-by-one & bygones & sit-up-straight & whisper in my ear & fluoride & figments of figments of figments & park it here & square root & after all & who's to tell & the drum has a hole & My goodness – Your badness & they-all-fall-down & down & down & The drum & The bet & The utter & butt & Bute & butter & who will tell & screams from the mountains & Ain't-it-the-truth?! & Hum with me baby & Come with me baby & Moan with me baby & Home with me baby & make it end – make it go away

& hopscotch & merry month of May & sniffle & puke & puddle & poodle & pick the lock & make it right & there's that scream again & the other & more from the attic & who's that coming? & Wait! The elusive among-us – Watch for the next one & . . . See what I mean? & The next one . . . To be sure . . . The other one . . . To be sure & . . . The next one & The Other one & . . . Too & . . . Too & . . . Too & Toot.

There's A Drum

After Anthony Tan's *Integration Ritual*

There's a drum beating down the road to oblivion. There's a drum touring the sky with abandon. No hesitation. There's a drum asleep at the edge of the lake. When we convince – when we converse – when we dialogue with others on our march to resurrect relics & broken promises. Why now, You ask & no one's here to answer. One corrupt occasion is no longer unique. Certainly. Not close to the one you seek. Too much time. Too little time. Not enough for these dizzying heights. When we count. When we discover. When we cogitate or even wonder. Will the kids cop to trouble afoot? Will we recover our love of compromise? Of resolution? Or is it now Revolution? First, the siren, then the ignition. There're fires in the hills. A divided sea. Urging salvation. Urging attention. One by one they trickle on. It's a lonesome road. At best. Listen. The siren again. Explosions unanswered. Bodies. Blankets. Our Bare essentials. Like Bigotry unhinged. Speak to us father. You who carry the drum. The question. The timid answers. Is this our dream? Our Nightmare? Our Destiny? Aloof & unframed. Watch. As the sky lightens . . . Is it always Safety First. A stringer of staggering strangers. Hear it? A Chorus. Unglued. Run-baby-Run. & The river finds new rhythm. Can we trust our presidents our wrinkled maps? & what-in-hell happened to remedy? To doubt? To remorse? Shuffle the cards & deal. One hand. One thought. One after another. He's stolen the sacred & the sublime. Hear the rustling in the wings. The tinkle of drumsticks against a blackened heart. Beat after beat. Step by step. Never the wiser. Never. The smallest among us fills the holes we've dug. & with that . . . Abstain? Confront? Or die? The choices are few & far between. Even his bitter lessons scatter as the storm-clouds brew, as grandmothers stitch the shrouds, as extraordinary evolves to ordinary – purity to poison.

Goya's

Disasters Of War

The Disasters Of War

1810-1820

The following poems were inspired by Francisco De Goya's 19th century etchings - *The Disasters Of War*

"Fatal consequences of the bloody war in Spain with Bonaparte, and other emphatic caprices" *Francisco de Goya - 1820*

"Haunting, macabre, and poignant, this series of 82 etchings known as "The Disasters of War" is a powerful reminder of the inhumane consequences of war . . . Goya sought to convey the tragic results of violent conflict through (these) harsh, realistic etchings. . . . The year is 1808, Napoleon installs his brother, Joseph as Spain's new ruler. The Spaniards refuse to accept his reign and on May 2, 1808, the Spanish War of Independence begins. This uprising became a part of the Peninsular War, which lasted until 1814. The conflict was the bloodiest event in Spain's modern history, with 215,000 to 375,000 Spanish military personnel and civilians dying during the war."

Posted January 9, 2019 In Art & Gallery News

Hola! Old friend . . .You, whose vision I've chased for years . . . As one from the plains who bears witness with his hands & blood in his throat . . .who speaks of the evil that men do & of the caller who knocks at every door . . .

Each day the donkey bears its burden of greed but *here* in Goya's 'night of the soul'

the corrupt haul each other on their backs & hurl their spears & pierce their own plump cocoons &

the dead will carry the dead / here where his monsters gorge on the torsos of kids & his priests walk a tightrope between their lies &

elegant women tease & flirt & are wrenched from their mother's tit & *here* a raging stallion tears her flesh &

she'll wear a mask to hide her scars & the hag will follow & sweep her up on a broom & sail over night &

here she'll feed on dragon's blood & dung & prefers a goat to a man & have him mount & . . . & *here*

the war tears out the country's throat & mutilates & castrates & ties the bleeding parts to a tree . . . & *here*

a women who plucks the teeth of the dead & dogs that gnaw the guts in the pit & *here* the headless corpses rot . . .

& Francisco de Goya will not be satisfied – *here* . . . & neither will we turn away . . . escape

the gapping & the gawking mouths . . . the grisly . . . hush.

Fundacio Caixa Catalunya [La Pedrera] – An Exhibition-Barcelona Spain - June 25, 2000

On his knees the lone man begs to be led away.

His wide white eyes stare into a sky all mottled & black.

He knows the future holds no salvation in the swirl of gas & scarlet rain.

Spitting blood but still with his knife he rushes the guns & gunners oblige

with bayonets & shot as they've done to the dead & dying

scattered below & beyond.

The ax-man hacks at belly & bone – his partner straddles another

driving his blade deep & down that grizzled

neck.

& now . . . The Women roil in rage w/thrust of sword or pike or

the heaving of stone – they joust & claw & bite, gouge

eyes from the skulls of the fallen.

Skirt stained with shit & blood of the fallen . . . & the seeping earth

/ she keeps

the cannon fire lit / turns night to day. 'Que Valor!'

calls. Goya.

The scream in the night / chant in the night: "They've taken the

women again.

To the bridge, to the camp. They've taken the women again."

& mothers w/daggers drawn &

brothers & fathers & nothing has changed.

They've tied your hands & covered your eyes so you cannot see

those who raise the rifles,

or him who ordered your death & hides in his bunker his

cock being sucked by

your wife or maybe your daughter too.

& if, as he, you'd come upon the dying & the dead you too may

vomit your guts & if

you'd witnessed, as he, the sodomy of his wife by the Captain &

his Sergeant-at-arms

you too would live shamed or beg to die.

Before rot / before buzzards / before the maggots bloom /

scavengers haul your dignity

away / leave you stripped & bare. Who you were

is insignificant: you are the naked & the dead.

& those who come to bury the fallen cannot remember 'why' or

'when' or even 'if'

there was reason. Their turn will come soon enough.

For Goya, it's "Enterrar y callar / Bury them & keep quiet."

The women who've been kept to satisfy the troops are useless on

the march. "There's

no more time," says one officer. "No more time to fuck around

boys. Do what must be

done. There are more down the road."

"We should treat them here?" "There's no time. Leave them for

Jose or Juan." "She's

bleeding from the rectum." "Leave them. There's no time" "He's

cut to the bowel.

I'm thinking peritonitis." "No! No time . . ."

& if you ask for your father you will be told to get to the field &

drag him off. It's

where they're stacked, they say. & the helpful one will tell you to

hurry before

the vultures & carpetbaggers & the wild pigs & . . .

"No se puede mirar*." But we do / at the prostrate & the huddled

& the prayerful &

the rifle barrels poised to fire but he will not show the men behind

the guns – it is

understood.

*One cannot look at this

come & butcher the fallen.

Where were they when their brothers fell & their neighbors /

when the pale

piano teacher was raped & disemboweled?

These naked bodies tossed to pit are a blessing. Before the rabble
 "Why & why is it?" "Why?" . . . Look. These men have tied their

rope to a tree & the noose

around his neck. Watch them / brace themselves / to yank

his head from his

bound body . . .

& & the two who have spread-eagled between them the naked body

of a man whose

prick & balls one hacks with his rapier while the militia muse minus

a glass or two

with which to toast.

There's no place for revolt. Your kitchen knife in the wrong hands

will bring death.

Even to priests. When shot they were still cassocked & bound &

each had his 'weapon'

dangling from his neck.

"Strange Fruit" this floppy body / Lady Day called it. & here,

in Goya's landscape,

it's amusement for a soldier who stops to admire the work of

compatriots / right to

those pants / dangling 'round his shit-stained shoes.

Long before gas in the trenches & 'Geneva' there was this: Naked,

mutilated body

of a prisoner impaled from rectum to neck on a branch in a tree.

& all around others /

carved to pieces . . .

If you don't want him to carry your visage to god or the devil, turn

him away / bind

him to the tree as if hugging it & then you & your cronies can riddle

him dead with

impunity.

In the end the victors take their time: First, the challenger

is slaughtered & stripped –

no dignity in death here – he's then . . . dismantled: head, legs,

arms, testicles & cock;

trophies strung from bush to branch.

& what of the citizens: who is left to cleanse & feed & quench the

fires that block

their retreat & what of the thieves & lechers; those who would sell

your soul as well

as your body?

Time comes for those left to shrivel & die. Nothing in the corral or

the field & no one

to be trusted / drained & withered / a faint wind to scatter the dust

that was their

bones.

Aftermath

In the end / the dead parade:

Harnessed one behind the other like a string of perch &

in his book the bat-winged scribbler enters their names to be

or not / honored by the host . . . & those left to rot are devoured

by the beasts Goya has set upon them & one owl he's kept for
himself

as monitor . . . & a hawk to mock the angels that will or will not

arrive in heaven . . . & the monster dog he's freed to regurgitate

what has become of the lives that were & are no longer . . .

Other Books By Roger Aplon

Stiletto
By Dawn's Early Light At 120 Miles Per Hour
It's Mothers' Day
Barcelona Diary
The Man With His Back To The Room
Intimacies
It's Only TV
Improvisations: Poetic Impressions From Contemporary Music
Mustering What's Left – Selected & New Poems 1976 – 2017
The Omnipotent Sorcerer

Chapbooks

Improvisations 1
Escapades
Homage To A Widow

www.ingramcontent.com/pod-product-compliance
Lightning Source LLC
LaVergne TN
LVHW051504170726
843492LV00002B/796